How to make soil and save **Earth**

by Allan Shepherd

photography: Giles Thaxton

with thanks to Louise Halestrap, Hele Oakley
and Suzanne Galant

© CAT Publications 2003
The Centre for Alternative Technology Charity Ltd.
Machynlleth, Powys, SY20 9AZ, UK
Tel. 01654 705980 Fax. 01654 702782
email: pubs@cat.org.uk Web: www.cat.org.uk
Registered Charity No. 265239.

ISBN 1 90217 516 6
1 2 3 4 5 6 7 8 9 10
Photography: Giles Thaxton

Mail Order copies from: Buy Green By Mail, Tel. 01654 705959.
The details are provided in good faith and believed to be correct at the time of writing,
however no responsibility is taken for any errors.
Our publications are updated regularly; please let us know of any
amendments or additions which you think may be useful for future editions.
Printed in Great Britain by Welshpool Printing Group Ltd.
on paper obtained from sustainable sources.

This book is brought to you by the **Centre for Alternative Technology**, or CAT for short. People often say, 'CAT? What's that all about?' and we struggle to give them a simple, snappy answer. This is because we're not doing something straightforward, like selling safety pins. We are a visitor attraction, a publisher, an educational facility, a mail order company, a membership organisation, and a centre for research. We like to produce books that combine all the different elements of our work, and *How to make soil and save Earth* is no exception. The composting techniques described here have been tried and tested by our biologists in a five-year programme of research. Part of the research was to ask people in our local area to try the techniques and we found that they worked very well. If you want to find out more about this research order *Cool Composting: a fresh approach* from www.cat.org.uk, or phone 01654 705959.

contents

This book is about composting **1**

A simple recipe for making soil and saving Earth **11**

The compost critters **15**

Beyond the kitchen **35**

Composting in small spaces **41**

Composting for one – worms and wormeries **53**

The average garden **57**

You don't want to do it like that **69**

Composting in large gardens **73**

Composting crises? What to do if your heap gives you the hump **95**

The directory **101**

This book is about composting

However much we've tried to disguise the fact in the title we can't get away from it. Why the subterfuge?

Composting has an image problem

And because of this most people don't do it.

Here are some great excuses not to compost anything in your life, ever; none of which would stand up in court:

- My garden has been stolen by aliens!
- I would, but I only wear white and composting is so dirty.
- I might start to enjoy it and that worries me because composting is just so un-cool, man.
- My grandad composts and he says it's a real art form.
- Composting; isn't that a winter sport?

The idea that composting is something somebody else does is about to change. Thanks to tough new environmental laws, composting will soon be as normal as breakfast. As most people don't want to think twice about breakfast, this book is for those who need compost making to be as simple as boiling an egg.

Most compost books start in the garden. This one starts in the kitchen…And doesn't get to the garden until page 39. This is because we think composting is as much about doing something constructive with rubbish (and most of our rubbish comes from or through the kitchen), as it is about making your garden grow. You don't have to be green-fingered to be green. You don't even need a garden. You just have to think that turning rubbish into soil, instead of sending it to a landfill site, is a good idea. And if you don't already think that, look at our 'lovely planet guide to landfill', overleaf, for some of the reasons why you should!

Lovely planet guide to landfill One of the least attractive landmarks on the planet is the landfill site. If you ever visit one – and, as 80 per cent of you live within 2km of one, this wouldn't be difficult – you will notice first of all the unusual sound-scape. This is created by the many thousands of scavenging seagulls, and other common birds, which come in search of food every day. Although the birds have been attracted by the plentiful food supply, many of them will suffer injury or slow death as they try to separate food items from the other rubbish. Hard to avoid, too, are the rats – no one knows how many there are in landfill, but we do know one pair can produce a colony of 2,000 rats in one year!

One of the most important and more constant activities on the landfill site is, however, sadly invisible – methane gas release. Methane is a powerful greenhouse gas – about twenty times more effective than carbon dioxide at creating global warming – so if you could see it, or any of the other 200 substances to be found in landfill gas, it would probably look impressive. So all praise to the humble kitchen scrap, without which British landfill would offer none of these great (un)attractions.

A simple recipe for making soil and saving Earth

I said that this book would make composting as simple as boiling an egg, and it will, but even Delia Smith has a recipe for boiling eggs, so let's start with a recipe. First of all find a container. Any container will do but some are better than others.

We recommend a neat and tidy box with a lid on top and a compostable bag inside (these can be ordered from CAT). However, the important thing here is turning rubbish into soil – so if you want to be avant-garde go for it, use whatever turns your handle. If you follow our recipe for making soil, this box, or 'kitchen caddy' as we call it, will play temporary host to about half a tonne of rubbish every year (if you're ten stone that's seven times your body weight!).

The compost critters

This cheese sandwich is our inspiration for compost making. But before I say why, I need to give you a quick biology lesson. I'm sorry but there's just no getting round it. The truth is you can't make soil on your own. You need help from other beings, millions of them: for simplicity's sake, let's call them compost critters.

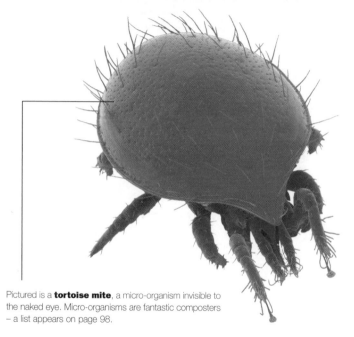

Pictured is a **tortoise mite**, a micro-organism invisible to the naked eye. Micro-organisms are fantastic composters – a list appears on page 98.

Compost critters eat rubbish and turn it into compost. They, like us, need a healthy diet (a nice balance of carbohydrates, proteins, fats, vitamins and minerals), suitable living conditions and plenty of air and water to survive. If you want to make soil you have to look after the compost critters.

Critters in the kitchen?

If you're worried about compost critters making a nice home for themselves in your kitchen, don't be. They won't. Compost critters don't invade your current rubbish bin and they won't bother with your kitchen caddy either.

The biology lesson over, let's get back to home economics. The picture of the cheese sandwich showed off a nice bit of Welsh cheese sandwiched between two slices of freshly baked wholemeal bread from our bakery in Machynlleth. This shows us what we must feed our compost critters – not literally two pieces of bread and a nice slab of cheese, but one foodstuff that is rich in carbohydrates and one that is rich in protein.

As we all know, cheese is a good source of protein and compost critters need protein to thrive. Luckily for us we don't have to feed them the cheese from our sandwich – although of course they will eat it if you do. Instead they can have kitchen scraps – peelings, skins, cores, the tops and bottoms of carrots, the sprouts the kids left on the side of the plate, the lettuce leaves you didn't fancy the look of, the tomatoes you found at the back of the fridge – all those food scraps, in fact, that normally find their way into the wheelie bin.

Although compost critters can eat a healthy wedge of protein, they cannot live on cheese alone. Like us, they need good healthy servings of starchy carbohydrate too. In fact they need much more carbohydrate than protein. In our cheese sandwich analogy the freshly baked bread represents carbon rich rubbish: in other words, paper and card…cereal packets, those small boxes containing the raisins your kids will eat, the box from the bumper pack of cream puffs you fancied the look of, the paper wrapper from the last packet of Moroccan figs you found at the back of the corner shop – all those papery things that normally find their way into the wheelie bin.

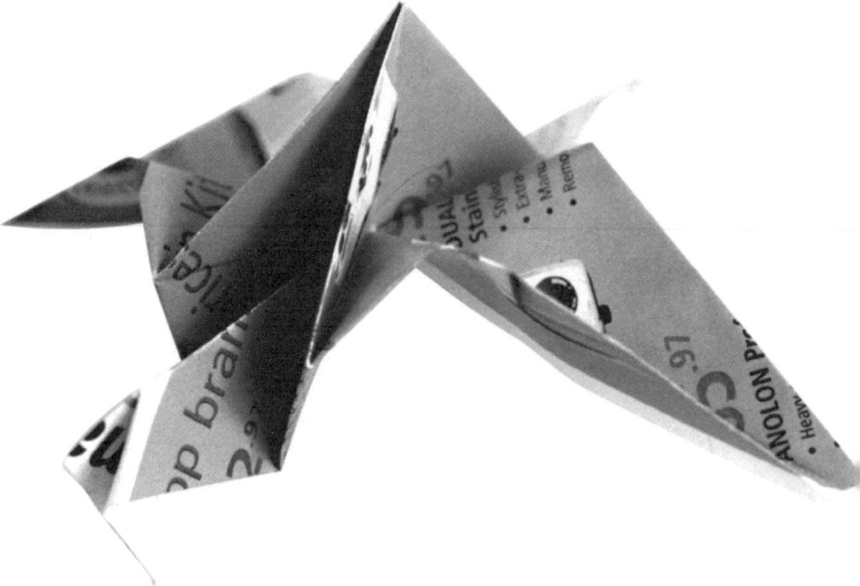

Even that origami kit your auntie bought you for Christmas…

Just feed and forget

This is the great thing about our compost method. It suits most people's lifestyles perfectly!

Compost critters need a home. They love air spaces. Some rubbish is already in perfect shape – crumpled tissues, paper towels and egg boxes for example. Don't bother cutting up cardboard boxes, compost critters prefer them crumpled. Rough them up a little – give them a quick squeeze. Scrunched balls of cardboard between the size of an egg and a small melon are ideal. Some things just don't compost, so don't bother putting them in your kitchen caddy. Non-biodegradable materials like metals, plastics, textiles and rubber are the obvious examples, but newspapers and magazines are better off in the recycling bin, too.

Compost critters don't like landfill sites. They don't find the right mix of protein and carbohydrate, and don't find nice pockets of air and supplies of fresh water. Instead they are squashed flat and are forced to live among toxic paints and batteries as well as metals, glass etc. They are squashed and waterlogged out of existence.

The landfill site is not completely devoid of life but the critters that take over are not composters. Landfill critters do eat kitchen scraps but they are eighteen times slower at it than compost critters. They also breathe out methane and carbon dioxide – both harmful greenhouse gases that create global warming – and sulphur dioxide (which smells like bad eggs). They also leave behind a putrid soup, which mixes in with toxic liquids.

Beyond the kitchen

Speaking of things left behind, it's time to get out of the kitchen.

Following the first part of our recipe is easy. To recap, take a container and fill it with food scraps and scrunched up cardboard and paper.

At some point your kitchen caddy is going to start overflowing. This is a tell-tale sign that it's time to empty it. If you've got a garden there's no mystery about where the contents can go. If you haven't you need to ask yourself some questions. For example, do I really want to have the view from my backyard recliner obliterated by a compost bin? If you've no space at all outside, you could donate the contents of your bin to a friend or neighbour who does, seek out or start a community composting scheme or persuade the council to start a doorstep collection scheme (see page 104).

The Great Outdoors So here we are on page 39 and, as promised, we can at last enter the garden, backyard, balcony or large window box.

Composting in small spaces

It's easy to compost in a backyard or balcony. In some respects it's easier than composting in the garden. For one thing you don't have lots of garden rubbish to get rid of – stuff like leaves, grass clippings and so on. However you will have other issues – the most obvious one being visual impact. Compost bins can be quite beautiful but some are just plain ugly – and the size of a small car. If you are composting only household waste you'll want something that is small, attractive and does the job quickly. Here are a few examples of bins we have on display at the CAT visitor centre. With affection, we call them the 'usual suspects'.

Name: Green Cone

Dimensions: 70 cm high

Capacity: 45 litres

Features: Its size means it will fit comfortably into the smallest garden space. Its unique mesh basket (which has to be sunk into the ground) means the kitchen and garden rubbish disappears straight into the soil. However, sometimes rats can chew through the mesh and take away the rubbish too. Unfortunately you can't use it in a yard or on a balcony. The Green Cone does not work well with our feed and forget system as it does not compost cardboard easily.

Available from: Green Cone

Name: The Bakre Composter

Dimensions: 80 cm high; 67 cm diameter

Capacity: 54 litres

Features: An easily assembled flat-packed bin with large aeration holes. Made from recycled plastic. Additional panels can be easily added to increase size, or removed to access compost.

Available from: Homebase

Name: Tiger Worm Composter

Dimensions: 37 cm high; 52 cm diameter

Capacity: 2 x 45 litres

Features: Designed to be a clean, efficient and compact composter for kitchen waste. The composter comes as a pair of bins with 1,000 red/tiger worms. The bins are made from compressed recycled newspaper and card. It works, but it's not rodent proof – it helps to place each bin on some bricks. Also, as it is designed especially for worms, you can't use our standard feed and forget system (see page 53 for the low-down on worms). Suitable for a single person or a small family.

Available from: Recycle Works

Name: Can-O-Worms

Dimensions of each tray: 73 cm high; 50 cm diameter

Capacity: 15 litres

Features: A tray structure allows easy access to the compost and the liquid is collected from a tap in the raised base. Designed specially for worms, so you can't use our standard feed and forget system. See page 53 for the low-down on worms.

Available from: CAT

Name: Original Wormery

Dimensions: 78 cm high; 24 cm wide; 17 cm deep

Capacity: 90 litres

Features: This bin has a dual chamber with aeration vents, an easy turn tap and a double seal lid. Designed specially for worms, so you can't use our standard feed and forget system. See page 53 for the low-down on worms.

Available from: Wiggly Wigglers

Composting for one – worms and wormeries

Worms are one of the great composters. They turn rubbish into soil very quickly. They eat rubbish (about half their own body weight everyday) and excrete worm casts (a high quality compost). There is a price to pay for this efficiency and the price is convenience. You can't feed and forget a wormery. Worms kept in a wormery are fussy pets. If you leave them for a weekend without enough food they can die. If you do go away you'll have to get a sitter for the worms and leave good instructions. They don't like acidic foods, e.g. citrus fruits, so if you have room for only one compost bin and you've chosen a wormery you'll have to throw some skins and peelings in the wheelie bin. You also need to buy in the worms. The common garden earthworm will not survive in a wormery because it is a deep burrower. Having said this the tiger, or brandling, worms that like wormeries are not particularly expensive and once you've bought them in you won't have to buy them again – so long as you look after them well. You can buy them from most wormery suppliers, or even from your nearest fishing shop. They breed prolifically, but only if there is a need to keep worm levels up. You won't have to worry about having too many because it won't happen.

Serving suggestion Lots of people ask the question – what do I do with my compost or 'soil' when I've made it? This is quite easy. Compost can be applied to borders or raised beds, used to pot up plants or added to your houseplants (so long as you let any compost critters escape before you do). Compost added to the garden improves the plant's chances of success. It enriches the condition of the soil so the plant can more easily find the nutrients it needs to thrive. Just like humans and compost critters, plants need a good balanced diet; lots of air, water and nutrients.

The average garden

The average garden is big enough to house a compost bin comfortably, but small enough to make it visible from any point in the garden or the house. This means that you'll want something that looks good and does the job too. Councils quite often give away compost bins, or sell them at a massive reduction, but you won't be able to choose the bin you really want.

Name: Wooden Modular Compost Bin

Dimensions: 75 cm high; 91 cm diameter

Capacity: 753 litres

Features: According to the manufacturer this bin takes only four minutes to erect. There are 'no nails, no screws and no holes to dig'. Because it is modular you can add to it as your addiction to composting grows.

Available from: CAT and Recycle Works

Name: Thermo Composter

Dimensions: 200 litres: 80 cm high; 54 cm diameter
2000 litres: 113 cm high; 178 cm diameter

Features: Modular bin can be enlarged, with a large hatch to empty compost. Made from recycled plastic.

Available from: Peter Ridley

Name: Blackwall Compost Tumbler

Dimensions: 105 cm high; 52 cm diameter

Capacity: 200 litres

Features: This bin is designed to make 'turning' easy, as it swings on a stand from a vertical to a horizontal position, making emptying easy too. Although turning is useful in hot composting systems it is not necessary in our feed and forget system.

Available from: Blackwall Ltd

Name: Milko Home Composter

Dimensions: 95.5 cm high; 80 cm diameter

Capacity: 290 litres

Features: Special aerating base, large rodent proof hatch for compost removal and adjustable ventilation.

Available from: CAT

Lawns and borders If your garden is like most gardens – with a lawn and borders – most of your compost will be made up of protein rich grass clippings and weeds. It is better for the lawn to leave the grass clippings where they fall but neatness gets the better of most of us. If you're adding plenty of carbohydrates (crumpled paper and card) from the kitchen to your bin, the addition of all this grass shouldn't be a problem.

Waiting time This is no speed race. Your compost will come when it comes and (unless you are in a particular hurry) the normal waiting time of between six months and a year is fine for most people. If you need to buy in compost before yours is ready, then look for some of the many environmental composts that are available. Avoid peat products because the harvesting of peat can lead to the destruction of valuable wildlife habitats. Try to go organic and look out for composts made from recycled waste. Local councils sometimes turn garden rubbish into a saleable compost. Contact the Compost Association for an approved list of suppliers and have a look at the small selection on pages 104 to 105.

You don't want to do it like that

If you have the misfortune to live next door to a gardening bore, you may be in for a bit of an earbashing. Experienced gardeners love to 'help' novices get to grips with gardening, but your well meaning neighbour may muddy the water by giving you the wrong advice for you and your chosen composting recipe. Our recipe keeps the compost cool because we want to provide a good home for compost critters. Some gardeners like their heaps hot. There's nothing wrong with this but the two recipes do not work together, so when you hear that familiar voice calling your name across the garden fence on a summer's day remember our special, 'You don't want to do it like that,' sample conversation. Here's how your chat might pan out…

Gardening Bore (GB): I see you're getting into composting.

You: That's right. I've just—

GB [before you can finish your sentence]: I hope you're getting it nice and hot in there.

You: Well, actually no. This is a new method called cool composting.

GB Cool composting! That doesn't sound right. I've been making compost for years and there's nothing better than a bit of hot composting. Do you want to know how to make it?

GB [before you have chance to answer]: You want to make a layer of nitrogenous waste [protein rich rubbish, such as kitchen scraps and grass cuttings to the likes of you and me] and then on top of it make a layer of carbon waste [carbohydrate rich cardboards and paper]. After a few days it's really hotting up. I've had it so you can brew tea in there.

[GB points to a large steaming mass of compost with a fair amount of straw and animal manure in it and the top of a Thermos flask poking out of the top].

You: Do you get many worms in there?

GB: Worms. Too hot for worms! It's fungi and bacteria that does my composting. In fact they create the heat, just by reproducing and consuming so fast. Of course, after a week or so they either cook themselves to death or run out of air or food.

You: Doesn't that slow things up?

GB: Aaah! I have a thermometer in there and when the temperature gets to dropping I just turn the heap over and it gets up high again.

You: [staring at GB's biceps]: Lot of work that?

GB: Oh I only turn it once a week. Doesn't take me more than an hour. I'll do yours if you like.

You: No, it's OK. I just feed and forget.

At this point GB will try and convince you to change your composting habits but don't give in. GB is trying to make as much compost as possible in the fastest time possible. Nothing wrong with this and you might get so into composting you'll want to be a hot heap speed freak too. But you'll have to spend a lot more time on your heap and this is one of the reasons we think compost is a dish best served cold.

Composting in large gardens

So, you've mastered our simple recipe for composting, you've seen how all living beings are connected by diet and you've taken a spiritual journey that has led you to take up a massive mortgage on a new house with a big garden. You think it couldn't happen to you? Here's three famous people who were known for other stuff before they took the same spiritual journey and became famous all over again for gardening:

Kim Wilde	**past:** pop singer responsible for eighties pop classic 'Kids in America'
	present: garden designer, TV gardener and garden writer
Monty Don	**past:** used to design jewellery and ran a very successful business
	present: face of BBC Gardeners' World
Tim Smit	**past:** show business entrepreneur
	present: created internationally famous garden attractions The Lost Gardens of Heligan and The Eden Project

Whatever the size of your larger garden you will have three new considerations: more grass clippings, wood prunings (unless you have no trees or shrubs) and leaves (ditto). You will also need to get a larger compost bin or bins. As we said earlier, you can buy bins the size of a small car but with your zest for gardening you might want to make your own (see pages 86 to 89).

Grass Grass is protein rich, so you'll need to keep topping the heap up with carbohydrate rich substances to make the cheese sandwich ratio balance out. If you get the balance wrong you'll start to notice that the compost is going off in a rather nasty way. If you've got a lot of woody waste around you can kill two birds with one stone by chipping it first and then putting it onto your compost heap. This will stop it going off and get rid of the wood.

Wood Green woody waste – that which is freshly cut – contains quite a lot of protein but it will still add carbohydrates to the heap. Old wood (cut twelve months before) has more carbohydrate, so you could leave it for a year and get a long term composting system going.

Mechanical chippers are quite common these days and you can get a good variety of sizes. You can hire them (look in the *Yellow Pages*): so plan for a couple of winter day's chipping every year and you'll save on the purchase and maintenance of an owned machine. Some councils are starting up shredding rounds, so phone and see if your local council has one.

Leaf mould Leaf mould is the simplest composting process of all and the large garden affords the luxury of having a separate pile. Most people just run some chicken wire round four posts, chuck the leaves inside the square and leave it. Fungi eat the leaves and break them down into useable compost within about a year. You can put leaves in a standard compost bin but leave the lid off because the leaves need to be damp. You could create some nice rustic leaf containers with chicken wire and some of the larger branches of woody waste that are lying about the place, but if you don't want the bother of making them you can buy them like that too. Leaves contain a good amount of carbohydrate so some people pile them up with the grass clippings to create a good carbohydrate/protein mix. This usually speeds up the composting process but demands more space.

Easy Build DIY Bin Number One:
The used tyre stack

Pros: Free, easy to put together, easy to empty, can make extra bins as required, rat proof.

Cons: Doesn't look very good, can be toppled over by kids or large dogs, small capacity.

Easy Build DIY Bin Number Two:

The pallet bin

Pros: free, quick and easy to build, big, can be multiplied, easy access for turning.

Cons: looks rough, compost can fall through gaps, not rat proof.

Easy Build DIY Bin Number Three:

New Zealand bin

Pros: neat appearance, removable front for access, easy to make in pairs, requires little skill.

Cons: needs bought timber, likely to rot.

Easy Build DIY Bin Number Four:

One tonne sack

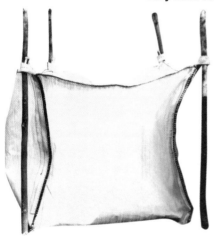

Pros: free from most skips and building sites, easy to set up, excellent for leaf compost.

Cons: can be floppy, not rat proof, difficult to empty.

Name: Eco Composter

Dimensions: 90 cm high; 90 cm diameter

Capacity: 708 litres

Features: It's big and has a big front hatch for taking out the compost. Made from recycled plastic.

Available from: Synprodo Plantpak Ltd

Name: David Bamford Bin

Dimensions: 100 cm high; 100 cm diameter

Capacity: 1,000 litres

Features: It's big and durable with a neat front hatch for taking out the compost. Made from recycled plastic. It's very heavy and the plastic warps over time.

Available from: David Bamford Recycled Plastics

Composting crises? What to do if your heap gives you the hump

If your compost starts to go off in a rather unpleasant way you know your bin's diet has gone off balance and you need to add more cardboard and paper. If you're mowing your lawn once a week and adding the grass clippings to the compost, you're going to be looking at your bin regularly anyway. This is your chance to have a quick look lower down in the heap to see how your compost critters are getting on.

You might have to get your hands deep into the compost to see what's going on but it will be worth it. Many of the compost critters (the bacteria, mites, and nematodes) are pretty much invisible but you should be able to get a good gawp at some of the bigger ones. If you can't see a good variety of the following you may have a problem: worms, woodlice, millipedes, springtails, slugs, ants, insect larvae, centipedes, straphylinid beetles.

It might be that your compost heap is too young but if it's been going for a few months the compost critters should be moving in. If they're not it might be time to think about your carbs:protein balance. The ideal is roughly equal proportions of carbohydrate and protein. But remember that you are not trying to create perfect compost, just the right sort of environment for your critters. And, believe it or not, critters aren't so fussy that they worry about precise ratios.

Those compost critters in full

Ants, Centipedes, Flat top mites, Fly larvae, Funghi, Millipedes, Mites, Astigmata mites, Beetle mites, Predatory mites, Tortoise mites, Nematodes, Protozoa, Pseudoscorpians, Slugs, Sow bugs, Spirochetes bacteria, Springtails, Staphylinidae beetles, Woodlice, Worms.

the directory

Compost Bins

Centre for Alternative Technology
www.cat.org.uk,
CAT, Machynlleth, Powys SY20 9AZ
Tel. 01654 705959
CAT sells kitchen caddies, Recycle works'
Modular Bin and Wiggly Wigglers' Wormery.
Also sells Ecosac compostable bags to fit
in the kitchen caddy.

Recycle Works
www.recycleworks.co.uk
Unit 1, Bill Mill, Ribchester,
Nr Longbridge PR3 3XJ
Tel. 01254 820088
Wooden Modular Compost Bin, Leaf Mould
Compost Bin, Tiger Worm Composter, Maxi
Waste Buster, Midi Waste Buster, Mini
Waste Buster.

Wiggly Wigglers
www.wigglywigglers.co.uk
Wiggly Wigglers, Lower Blakemere,
Herefordshire HR2 9PX
Tel. 01981 500391
Selection of wormeries, worms and
accessories.

Blackwall Limited
www.blackwall-ltd.com
Seacroft Estate, Coal Road,
Leeds LS14 2AQ
Compost Converter, CompostABin,
Compost Tumbler, Soil Saver.

Green Cone

www.greencone.com
3rd Floor, 58 Grosvenor Street,
London WlK 3JB
Tel. 020 7499 4344
email: headoffice@hogreencone.com
The Green Cone System,
The Green Cone Kitchen Caddy.

Gone Gardening Limited

www.gonegardening.com
Simon Woodhead
Tel. 08451 300100
Britannia Composter Round, Britannia
Composter Square, Eco-composter 180.

Peter Ridley Waste Systems

www.peterridley.co.uk
Crown House, Gt. Glemham,
Saxmundham, Suffolk IP17 2DJ
Tel. 01728 663395
Thermo composters.

Plysu Recycling

Wolseley Road, Kempston,
Bedford K42 7UD
Tel. 01234 841771
220 Garden Composter.

First Tunnels

www.firsttunnels.co.uk
Dixon Street, Barrowford,
Lancashire BB9 8PL
Tel. 01282 601253
Composter 330, Composter 170,
Compost Tumbler.

Keengardener Ltd
T/A CMS Gardens

www.cmsgardens.co.uk
19 Arden Centre, Arden Road,
Alcester, Warwickshire B49 6HW
Tel. 01789 763336
The Beehive Composter
– 5 painted variations.

Harcoster Garden Products

www.harcoster.co.uk
Windover Road, Huntingdon,
Cambridgeshire PE29 7EE
Tel. 01480 445113
280 litre composter, 200 litre composter.

Bins N Benches

www.bins-n-benches.freeserve.co.uk
Smithy Lane, Holmeswood,
Ormskirk, Lancashire L40 1UH
Tel. 07831 589103
The Forrest Composter, Rotating Barrel
Composter, Leaf Mould Composter.

Home Composting Project

www.compost-it.org
Unit 5, Creswell Business Park, Colliery
Road, Creswell, Worksop S80 4BX
Tel. 01909 722055
Soil Saver 325 litres.

Original Organics

www.originalorganics.co.uk

Unit 9, Langlands Business Park,
Uffculme, Cullompton,
Devon EX15 3DA
Tel. 01884 841515
Rotal Classic and Rotal 220, The Original
Wormery, The Junior Wormery.

David Bamford Recycled Plastics

Tel. 01544 267849
The David Bamford Bin.

Synprodo Plantpak Ltd

www.plantpak.co.uk
Burnham Road, Mundon, Maldon,
Essex CM9 6NT
Tel. 01621 745500
Large Eco-Composter.

Linpac Environmental

www.linpac-environmental.com
Leafield Way, Leafield Industrial Estate,
Corsham, Wilts SN13 9UD
Tel. 01225 816500
220 and 330 litre composters.

Composting organisations

Community Composting Network

67 Alexandra Road, Sheffield S2 3EE
Tel/Fax. 0114 2580483
email. ccn@gn.apc.org
Provides advice and support to new and existing community composting projects across the UK. Contact to receive their free information pack.

The Composting Association

www.compost.org.uk
Avon House, Tithe Barn Road,
Wellingborough,
Northamptonshire NN8 1DH
email. membership@compost.org.uk
The Composting Association is the UK's membership organisation that researches and promotes best practice in composting and the uses of composts. The Association acts as a central resource for composting, researching, collecting and disseminating information.

Henry Doubleday Research Association

www.compost-uk.org.uk
Coventry, Warwickshire, CV8 3LG
Tel. 024 7630 8202
Fax. 024 7630 8225
Carries out research and provides advice on composting as a sustainable solution to organic waste management.

Buying in compost

Most garden centres stock a range of peat free composts and some will have organic composts (a comprehensive list of approved composts is available from the Compost Association). Here's a list of peat free composts recommended by Friends of the Earth.

- B&Q peat-free multipurpose compost
- Fertile Fibre products
- Homebase peat-free multipurpose compost
- J Arthur Bowers
- Levington
- Shamrock

- TERRA EcoSystems
- Wessex
- Westland

If you can't get hold of the compost you want at a garden centre try one of the following mail order suppliers.

B&Q DIY Stores
www.diy.com
Supplies peat-free compost which can be ordered online. Products include potting compost, sowing and cutting compost and Shamrock multipurpose coir (coconut fibre) compost.

Crocus
www.crocus.co.uk
Supplies a range of composts and mulches including Levington and J. Arthur Bowers reduced peat composts.

Fertile Fibre
www.barrett.org.uk/fertilefibre/prices.html
Soil Association certified, Organic, peat-free potting and seed composts, plus organic fertilisers & feeds, mulches and coir blocks. Delivery throughout mainland UK.

Gone Gardening
www.gonegardening.com/gg_shop
Supplies a range of composts including Levington peat-free and Westland organic compost.

Homebase DIY Stores
www.homebase.co.uk
Supply a number of composts and some peat-free growing soils.

Barker & Bland, Purveyors of Fine Composts and Manures
www.dalefootcomposts.co.uk
Barker & Bland produces and supplies 'Lakeland Gold', a well balanced, peat-free soil conditioner full of rich organic material.

William Sinclair Horticulture Ltd
www.william-sinclair.co.uk
Supplies J Arthur Bowers and Sinclair compost products.

Composting books

All of the following books are available from CAT. For full details visit www.cat.org.uk or phone 01654 705959 for our mail-order catalogue.

Cool Composting, CAT, £3.50
Worm Composting, HDRA, £2.00
Composting for All,
Nicky Scott, Green Books, £1.95
Gardening with compost,
F.C.King, Plum Tree, £9.99
The Compost Book,
David and Yvonne Taylor, Hale, £3.99
Worms Eat My Garbage,
Mary Applehof, Flower Press, £8.95
Rodale Book of Composting,
Rodale, £10.95
Backyard Composting,
John Roulac, Green Earth Books, £4.95
The Soul of Soil, Joe Smiley and Grace Gershing, Chelsea Green, £11.95
All About Compost,
Pauline Pears, HDRA, £6.95

Recycling – The final word

Now you're separating your food scraps from the rest of your rubbish it's only a little more effort getting into recycling. Here is a list of great organisations who'll re-use your rubbish or find people who can use the stuff you don't want any more.

Cars

Ebony Solutions UK

www.ebony-solutions.co.uk
Northwich, Cheshire
Tel. 01606 301222,
Fax. 01606 301320
email. ediesel@ebony-solutions.co.uk
Make bio-diesel from recycled vegetable oil donated by the public.

Oil Recycling Association

1 Burrowfields, Basingstoke,
Hampshire RG22 4XJ
Tel. 01256 840049,
Fax. 01256 840049

Member companies of the association provide oil and garage waste recycling services.

Tyre Collection Services Ltd

www.tyrecollection.com
Parkway North, Western Way,
Wednesbury, W. Midlands WS10 7BW
Tel. 0121 556 3493
Fax. 0121 556 9751
email. info@tyrecollection.com
TCS offers a nationwide service as the only national collector with regular, scheduled collection of used car, van, truck and agricultural casings.

Batteries

RABBITT Recycling Ltd

(Recycle All Batteries Bulbs Inkjet Toners & Telephones)
www.worktwice.co.uk/rabbitt
The Cottages, 27-29 New Street,
Charfield, Wotton-under-Edge,
Gloucestershire GL12 8ES
Tel. 0800 138 0988
Fax. 01453 521330
email. info@rabbittrecycling.co.uk
Worktwice Marketing Ltd, G & P Batteries Ltd and Mercury Recycling Ltd have put a scheme together for a single point collection and recycling of all types of batteries as well as toner and Inkjet cartridges, fluorescent tubes, light bulbs, mobile phones and obsolete computer hardware.

REBAT (Recycling Batteries)

www.rebat.com
BBMA, 26 Grosvenor Gardens,
London SW1W 0GT
Tel. 020 7838 4800
Fax. 020 7838 4801
REBAT is an initiative managed by the British Battery Manufacturers Association (BBMA) to encourage collection of nickel cadmium (NiCD) batteries in the UK under European legislation. Contains a comprehensive list of contact details of

major battery /appliance manufacturers and distributors and information on battery disposal and collection schemes.

Books

The Prism Project
P.O. Box 6031, Bishops Stortford, Herts CM23 1PP
Tel. 01279 777007
Fax. 01279 777177
email. info@prismproject.org
Recycles books and tapes with self help themes by collecting donations and passing them on to prison inmates.

Paint

Community Re>Paint
www.communityrepaint.org.uk
C/o 74 Kirkgate, Leeds LS2 7DJ
Tel. 0113 243 8777
Fax. 0113 234 4222
email. mark@swap-web.co.uk
A unique waste minimisation/reuse initiative in Britain which diverts unwanted and surplus paint from the waste stream and redistributes it to community groups, charities and voluntary organisations. SWAP acts as the national co-ordinator for the project. Has links to contact details of local schemes.

Construction

SalvoWEB
www.salvo.co.uk
Tel. 01890 820333
Fax. 01890 820499
Directory of antique, reclaimed, salvaged, recycled, reproduction, replica, traditional, conservation, restoration, heritage, green, environmentally-friendly materials, craftspeople, restorers, dealers, makers for buildings and gardens.

Computer equipment and mobile phones

ActionAid
www.nru.org.uk
Unit 14 Kingsland Trading Estate,
St Philips Road, Bristol BS2 0JZ
Tel. 08453 100200
email. recycling@aarecycling.org.uk
ActionAid Recycling aims to reduce waste,
recycle, re-use and reduce poverty. Collects
empty toner and inkjet cartridges from
printers, faxes and photocopiers, and
unwanted mobile phones with free
collections throughout the UK. All profits
from recycling go to the charity ActionAid.

Child Advocacy International UK
www.child-advocacy-int.org
75a London Road,
Newcastle Under Lyme ST5 1ND
Tel. 01782 712599
Donates to the CRUMP – Campaign to
Recycle Unwanted Mobile Phones, or your
depleted inkjet printer cartridges for
recycling and helps raise funds for CAI UK.

ComputerAid International
www.cit.org.uk/computeraid
Unit 114 Belgravia Workshop,159
Marlborough Road, London N19 4NF
Tel. 020 7281 0091
Fax. 020 7281 0058
email. info@computeraid.org
Recycles computers from both consumers
and business for use by education, health
and community organisations in the
developing world.

Computers for the Disabled
www.cftd.co.uk
41 New Waverly Road, Noak Bridge,
Basildon, Essex SS15 4BJ
Tel. 01268 284834
Fax. 01268 284834
A volunteer run charity that repairs and
upgrades computers and supplies PCs,
software and parts to disabled people or
centres for the disabled.

Free Computers for Education

www.free-computers.org

Tel. 01932-874066

Free Computers for Education is a Registered Charity set up to collect computers that are no longer needed by industry, saves them from being smashed up and dumped in landfill sites, has them professionally refurbished, and then gives them free of charge to schools in need via local Rotary Clubs.

Mobilephones4charity

www.mobilephones4charity.com

Dorset House, Regent Park, Kingston Road, Leatherhead, Surrey KT22 7PL

Tel. 01372 824265

Fax. 01372 824306

email.admin@mobilephones4charity.com

Recycles redundant mobile phones (together with the battery and charger if possible) to raise funds for a charity of the donor's choice.

The Furniture Recycling Network (FRN)

c/o CFS, The Old Drill Hall, 17a Vicarage Street North, Wakefield WF1 4JS

Tel. 01924 375252

Fax. 01924 375252

email. furniture.rn@virgin.net

Umbrella network for around 300 furniture recycling projects in the UK. The public can donate unwanted furniture, a nearby project will collect it and it will be sold on to people on low incomes.

Textiles

Textile Recycling Association

www.textile-recycling.org.uk

P.O. Box 124, Huntingdon, Cambs PE18 7DP

Tel. 01480 455249

Fax. 01480 453680

email. tra@recyclemetals.org

Association website has a list of memebers and details including what materials are worked with.

Miscellaneous

In Kind Direct
www.inkinddirect.org
19 Milk Street, London EC2V 8AN
Tel. 020 7860 5930
Fax. 020 7860 5920
email. media@inkinddirect.org

In Kind Direct has a network of partner charities and smaller voluntary organisations all over the UK. Companies can donate surplus goods for redistribution, including office equipment and supplies, furniture, flooring, household appliances, linen & bedding, toiletries, books, toys, educational materials and clothing.

Junkfox
www.junkfox.com

10 Boundstone Road,
Farnham, Surrey GU10 4TQ
Tel. 01252 792040
Online facility for trading second-hand, antique or recycled items.

Reactivated.co.uk
www.reactivated.co.uk
13 Lime Street, Todmorden,
Lancashire OL14 5JN
Tel. 01706 810518
Fax. 01706 839913
Makes interesting home and office products from unwanted materials, from inner tubes and old agricultural machinery to CDs and OS maps. Currently seeking donations of scrap CDs for development of new products.

Re-cycle
www.re-cycle.org
60 High Street, West Mersea,
Essex CO5 8JE UK
Tel/Fax. 01206 382207
email. info@re-cycle.org

Re-Cycle's mission is to collect and ship second hand bicycles and parts to developing countries.

Tools for Self Reliance

www.tfsr.org

Netley Marsh Workshops, Netley Marsh, Southampton SO40 7GY

Tel. 02380 869697

email. info@tfsr.org

Helps grassroots development projects in Africa by providing refurbished hand tools and sewing machines. In the UK there are around 70 refurbishing groups and 100 tool collection points.

Vision Aid Overseas

www.vao.org.uk

12 The Bell Centre, Newton Road, Manor Royal, Crawley, West Sussex RH10 9FZ

Tel. 01293 535016,

Fax. 01293 535026

email. info@vao.org.uk

You can send your unwanted glasses to this registered charity dedicated to helping people in developing countries with bad eyesight, particularly in those cases where eyewear can help.

Acknowledgements

This book is the result of several years of research into CAT's own high fibre composting technique. During these years CAT staff carried out trials at our visitor centre, and with a wide variety of householders in our local area – the Dyfi Valley. They found that the high fibre composting method was very easy to carry out and provided good results. I would like to take this opportunity to thank all the individuals and organisations who provided funding for this research, including Hanson Landfills, JJ Sainsburys Charitable Trust, and an anonymous donor, and the following CAT staff who carried it out: Peter Harper, originator of the idea, head of research and innovation at CAT and writer of CAT factsheet Cool Composting: a fresh approach, Louise Halestrap (whose valuable advice and technical knowledge made this book possible), Judith Thornton, Mark Brown, Marcus Zipperlen and Corrine Bacon. I would also like to thank Hele Oakley and Suzanne Galant for additional research for this book.

Vascular Neurology
Board Review